IT'S CHRISTMAS

by Jack Prelutsky

pictures by
Marylin Hafner

SCHOLASTIC INC.
New York Toronto London Auckland Sydney

ISBN 0-590-40584-5

Text copyright © 1981 by Jack Prelutsky.
Illustrations copyright © 1981 by Marylin Hafner.
All rights reserved.
This edition published by Scholastic Inc.,
730 Broadway, New York, NY 10003,
by arrangement with Greenwillow Books,
a division of William Morrow & Company, Inc.

12 11 10 9 8 7   8 9/8 0 1/9

Printed in the U.S.A.   28

FOR JENNY AND ERIK,
MERRY CHRISTMAS!
-J. P.

FOR ABIGAIL, JENNIFER, AMANDA
-M. H.

CONTENTS

IT'S CHRISTMAS

It's Christmas! Merry Christmas!
Yes, it's merry, merry Christmas,
it's a time for hanging stockings,
it's a time for riding sleighs,
it's a time for jolly greeting,
snow and holly, overeating,
oh, I love you merry Christmas,
you're the best of holidays.

Dear Santa Claus,

It's me again
reminding you I'm here,
I'm making my list easier
and shorter than last year.

I'd like a stack of comic books,
a dozen apple pies,
a box of chocolate brownies,
and an elephant that flies,

a porpoise for the bathtub
and a dragon for my room,
a robot that does homework
and can also use a broom.

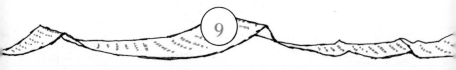

And I'd like a hippopotamus,
a trumpet, and a drum,
I could use a half a dollar
and a million sticks of gum.

Just leave them underneath our tree
or near our fireplace,
Oh! you probably won't bring them,
but I'm writing ... just in case.

OUR CHRISTMAS TREE

Daddy took me to the forest
for our Christmas tree today,
he said that we'd enjoy it
and we'd hardly have to pay.

We were wearing scarves and mittens,
all our very warmest clothes,
but our cheeks soon looked like cherries
and our fingers nearly froze.

We hunted through the forest
for a tree that was just right,
by the time we finally found one
we were both an awful sight,

I was shivering and shaking,
Daddy shook and shivered too,
I was colder than an iceberg,
Daddy's face was turning blue.

Daddy finally chopped that tree down,
but the way he did was dumb,
when it fell, it knocked him backwards
and he cut his nose and thumb,
Daddy also sprained his shoulder,
banged an elbow, scraped a knee,
as I helped him up, he muttered,
"Son! Next year we'll buy our tree."

THE MISTLETOE

Mommy,

Daddy,

quick!

Let's go

and stand

beneath

the mistletoe.

You kiss me

and I'll kiss you,

here comes Sister,

kiss her too.

Mommy,
Daddy,
quick!
Let's go
and stand
beneath
the mistletoe.

ANOTHER SANTA CLAUS

Christmas day will soon be here,
it must be so, because
no matter where I look, I see
another Santa Claus.

When our doorbell rang this morning,

it was Santa at the door,

and when we went Christmas shopping,

I saw Santa in the store.

There are Santas, lots of Santas,
in the windows brightly lit,
and on almost every corner
still more Santa Clauses sit.

SEASONS GREETINGS

20

I see Santas by the dozen,
by the million, by the ton,
how strange to see so many,
since there *can't* be more than one.

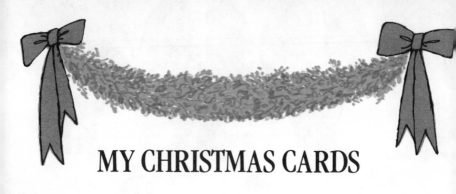

MY CHRISTMAS CARDS

Oh, no one got my Christmas cards,
it's making me upset,
I sent them off two weeks ago,
but no one got them yet.

I drew a bunch of pictures
and I wrote some poems that rhyme,
I sent them off *two weeks* ago,
that should be lots of time.

I mailed them to my cousins,
to my uncles and my aunts,
I sent them off TWO WEEKS ago,
I think they've had their chance.

But no one got my Christmas cards,

not Mommy and not Gramps,

I sent them off *TWO WEEKS* ago...

did I forget the stamps?

OUR CHRISTMAS PLAY

We were nervous and excited
in assembly today,
for our parents came to visit us
and watch our Christmas play.

Our teachers helped a little,
but we did the most ourselves,
the fattest kid played Santa
and the smallest kids were elves.

A few were Santa's reindeer
so they got to run and leap,
some of us were shepherds,
and a bunch were woolly sheep,

there was Jesus in the manger,
there were angels wearing wings,
there was Joseph, there was Mary,
and the three wise Eastern kings.

We wore makeup, we wore costumes,
it was really lots of fun,
and our parents all applauded
when our Christmas play was done,
then we took our bows together,
everyone that is, but me—

I just stood there, green and fragrant,
for I played the Christmas tree.

SINGING
CHRISTMAS CAROLS

On Christmas Eve we bundle up
and go out caroling,
our neighbors shut their windows
when they hear my family sing.

My voice is very beautiful,
I sing just like a bird,
but everybody drowns me out
so I am barely heard.

Dad sings like a buffalo
and Mother like a moose,
my sister sounds like breaking glass,
my brother like a goose.

Some people come and greet us,
they bring cookies on a tray,
I think they give us cookies
just to make us go away.

Though our singing sounds so sour
it sends shivers down my spine,
when we're caroling together
there's no family sweet as mine.

MAYBE THEY'LL GO AWAY!

TOMORROW IS CHRISTMAS

Tomorrow is Christmas,
I'm terribly sad,
my friends are all merry
but I'm very mad.

I'm feeling so awful
I hardly can speak,
I wish that this Christmas
would wait one more week.

I'm really unhappy,
I'm down in the dumps,
Tomorrow is Christmas
and I have the mumps.

A SLED FOR CHRISTMAS

UP! UP! Up I jump
and down the stairs I fly.
LOOK! LOOK! A brand new sled
that I can't wait to try.

ZIP! ZIP! Bundle up,

I'm toasty warm inside.

QUICK! QUICK! Out the door,

then down the hill I'll glide.

NO! NO! It isn't fair,
it simply isn't right.
SNOW! SNOW! I see no snow,
it melted overnight.

AUNTIE FLO

Every year on Christmas
there's a gift from Auntie Flo,
she's sent me pairs of underwear
for three years in a row.

The box is always beautiful,
the bow is neatly tied,
but I'm always disappointed
when I see those shorts inside.

I wish she'd send a model plane,
or even a big stuffed bear,
I'd take a box of stones and rocks,
but please! no underwear.

MY CHRISTMAS PUP

It's Christmas and I'm happy
'cause I got a little puppy,
it's a floppy little puppy
of my very, very own,
oh, he's hopping and he's skipping
and he's flopping and he's flipping
and he's sitting and he's nipping
on a little rubber bone.

Oh, his tummy's sort of tubby

and his tail is sort of stubby

and his head is sort of moppy,

oh, I love my little pup,

yes, I love my little puppy,

little tubby floppy puppy,

(even though he made a puddle

and I had to wipe it up).

JACK PRELUTSKY was born and raised in New York City but now lives in Albuquerque, New Mexico. He has been entertaining young readers for years with his funny and original books of poems, including *It's Halloween*; *It's Thanksgiving;* and three ALA Notable Books: *The Queen of Eene*, *The Snopp on the Sidewalk*, and *Nightmares*–a chilling collection of monster poems. He has also translated several books of German and Swedish verse, including *The Wild Baby* and *The Wild Baby Goes to Sea* by Babro Lindgren.

MARYLIN HAFNER studied at Pratt Institute and the School of Visual Arts in New York City. She has illustrated several distinguished children's books, including *The Crow and Mrs. Gaddy*, *The Candy Witch*, *It's Halloween*, and *It's Thanksgiving*–all available from Scholastic.